Celebrity Spice

Parveen K. Ahmed

GW01312868

Copyright 2013

acknowledgements.

I would like to dedicate this book to my son Hashim for all his hard work and determination and the unconditional love he has given me.

Firstly I wish to thank my husband Anjum for all his support and advice he has given. Thanks go to all Hashim's medical team at the Royal Manchester Children's Hospital, all my children, for being so patient when the kitchen was inundated with unexpected guests, the hospital charity team, the photographer Rick Milnes who gave his precious time and the celebrities who took part in this book. I am indebted to many people who have assisted me in various ways while I was working on this book- they'll know who they are! And finally, my angel from heaven Hazel Gardner- without her input and expertise the book would not have been possible.

A great big thanks to everyone!

contents.

Foreword..4

Kevin Moran- **Chicken with Spinach**.................................6

Dean Gorré- **Lamb Biryani**...8

Bear Grylls- **King Prawn Korma & Garlic Naan**.......................10

Jason Done- **Chicken Tikka Masala**................................12

Tupele Dorgu- **Chicken Korma**....................................14

Jimi Harkishin- **Keema Matr**.......................................16

Fiona Bruce- **Southern Indian Fish Curry**.........................18

Nigel de Jong- **Coconut Prawn Curry**.............................20

Mike Toolan- **Chicken Karahi**.....................................22

John Thomson- **Makhan Chara**....................................24

Amir Khan- **Karahi Chops**..26

Ray Ranson- **Chicken Bhuna**.....................................28

Julie Hesmondhalgh- **Vegetarian Balti Rogan Josh**.................30

Sir Richard Branson- **Chicken Pilau Rice**........................32

Sir Trevor McDonald- **Lamb Bhuna**...............................34

Gemma Atkinson- **Chicken Rogan Josh**............................36

Sir Michael Parkinson- **Bombay Potatoes**........................38

Leona Lewis- **Chickpea Curry**....................................40

John O'Shea- **Lamb Rogan Josh**..................................42

Sally Dynevor- **Matr Paneer**.....................................44

About the author..46

foreword.

Life is just not what you expect it to be, the strangest things can happen. In recent times, I have laughed, cried and experienced the surreal. I have found Coronation Street stars in my kitchen, chopping onions and stirring peas, side by side with Premiership football players. I have acquired a tremendous amount of quite unusual information. For example, Leona Lewis is a vegetarian and Sir Trevor McDonald loves lamb bhuna! Whilst chatting to Sir Michael Parkinson I discovered his liking for Bombay potatoes. I have been surprised by Bear Grylls- I would have put him down for a seriously hot vindaloo but he turned out to be a king prawn korma man. I have collected a kaleidoscope of celebrities to contribute their favourite curries for this book.

You may ask what brought all these characters together? The answer is one person and one event...

Saturday morning on a bright, spring day, March 29th

My busy, happy family home, five sons with hectic lifestyles, grabbing a quick breakfast and off to sporting activities. One son was still in bed. He had been at the doctor's the day before and had a diagnosis of tonsilitis. When I couldn't wake him I knew there was something terribly wrong. I tried to stay calm as I didn't want to panic the family. Within minutes, he had stopped breathing and I found myself on the phone to paramedics, while his older brother gave him mouth to mouth resuscitation the best way he could.

An unknown virus had come crashing into our lives, bringing brain injury with it. Within twenty four hours, my lively, sporty, funny and intelligent fourteen year old had become a vulnerable, seriously ill child on life-support and not expected to survive. Hashim was a "golden boy"- an ambitious adventurer who seemed blessed and managed to excel at everything he tried. We could barely recognise the young boy we saw us, wired up to machines and pumps.

Hashim was in the care of the Royal Manchester Children's Hospital. He was completely non-reactive and in a deep coma for eight weeks. While we waited for the swelling on the brain to go down, we prayed for him. He came out of the coma, unable to walk or feed himself. He communicated by blinking his eyes until some speech returned, and he was able to ask if this was real or if he was having a nightmare.

The care he received from a raft of dedicated professionals was truly outstanding. We were helpless and powerless as a family because we were out of our depth and completely in the hands of strangers- the medical staff. Their support was magnificent as they began the difficult task of rehabilitating Hashim. Nobody could predict a very positive outcome, but my son's powerful determination began to emerge and he stubbornly fought through a painful recovery- which is still ongoing.

When our son came home to us we were thrilled and very, very grateful. We felt we owed the hospital an enormous debt. I wanted to thank them by somehow helping them to continue their incredible work. Being a cookery teacher, I thought I would try to use my skills to raise money for the hospital. I usually give group cooking classes or instruct individuals, including one or two local celebrities. So I did what I do best- I cooked! I held a charity lunch and served everyone's faourite dish- the curry! In fact, I presented a selection of curries that went down extremely well, so well that people wanted the recipes and suggested I put them in a book. That was when the idea for this charity celebrity cookbook was born.

I then found myself on a whirlwind, rollercoaster ride trying to push forward a fundraising project for the hospital, and learned 'on the job'! I have asked numerous people for help in this endeavour and I have been constantly amazed by the kindness I have found. I have seen the best part of human nature, the part rarely discussed or celebrated, the willingness to help others. Every time I made a request in aid of vulnerable children, the basic, instinctive answer was always "yes".

So please enjoy this book, grab the ingredients and cook a celebrity's favourite curry. This really is a unique and delicious way to help a children's hospital!

Parveen K. Ahmed

'The Curry Queen'
curryqueen.co.uk

Kevin Moran
Chicken with Spinach

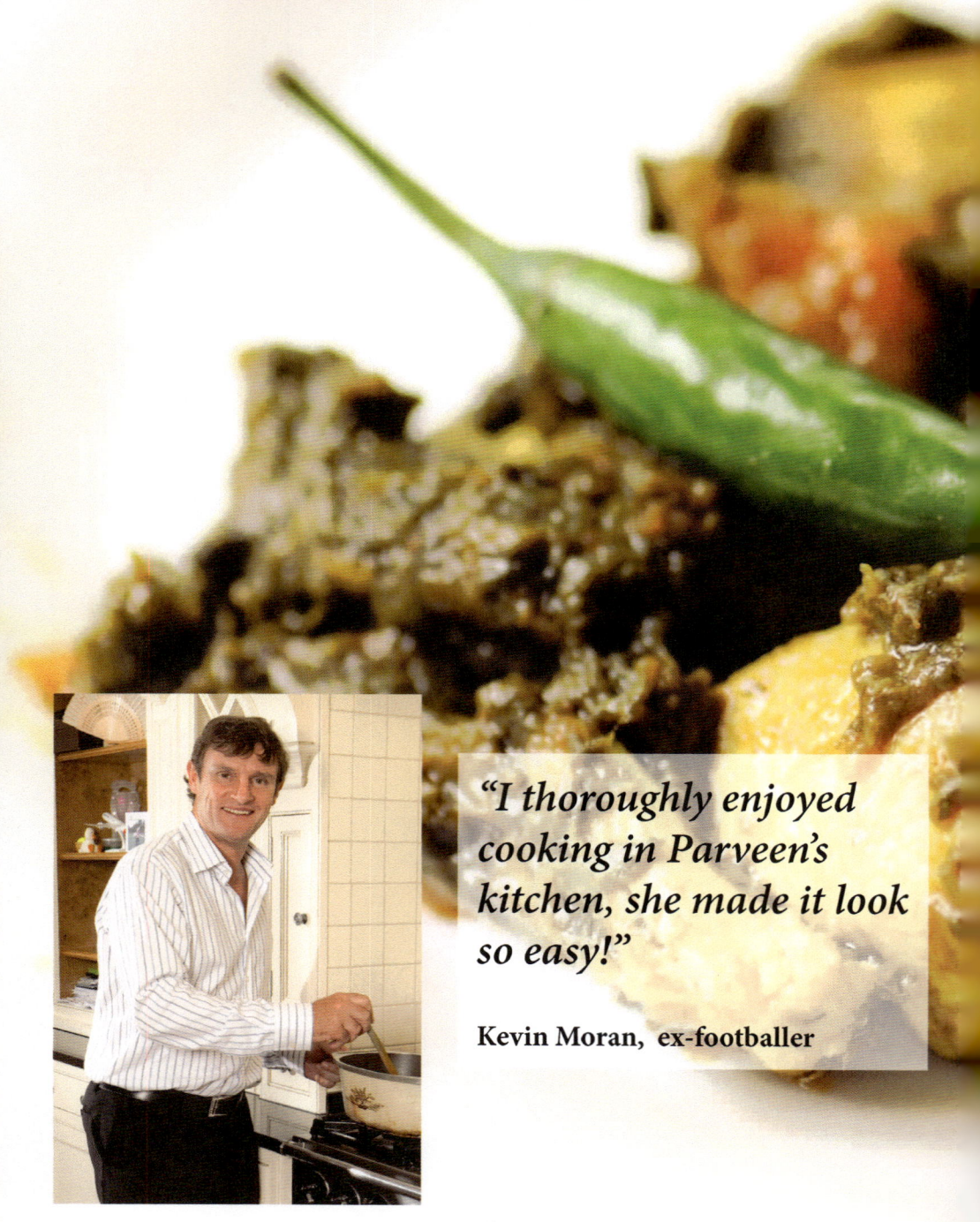

"I thoroughly enjoyed cooking in Parveen's kitchen, she made it look so easy!"

Kevin Moran, ex-footballer

Ingredients:

1 small chicken cut into pieces
Half a tin of chopped tomatoes
3 medium sized onions
1 tin of spinach purée or fresh spinach
3 tablespoons of milk
1 teaspoon of dill
Half a tablespoon of salt
Half a tablespoon of red chilli powder
Half a tablespoon of curry powder
1 teaspoon of black onion seeds
A pinch of jeera
5 cloves of garlic
A little fresh ginger
5 green chillies
A sprig of fresh coriander
3 tablespoons of olive oil
1 tablespoon of garam masala
A glass of water

Method:

1) Chop the onions and brown in the olive oil until golden brown.
2) Add the tomatoes, crushed garlic and ginger, all the chilli powder, salt, curry powder, jeera, black onion seeds and stir.
3) Add the washed chicken pieces with 1 glass of water. Put on full heat for 5 minutes.
4) Lower the heat and leave for 15 minutes to cook.
5) Increase the heat to full and "pun" the chicken.
6) In a separate pan add the spinach, dill and milk and let it cook well for 20 minutes.
7) Put the spinach into the chicken and add the coriander and garam masala to garnish.

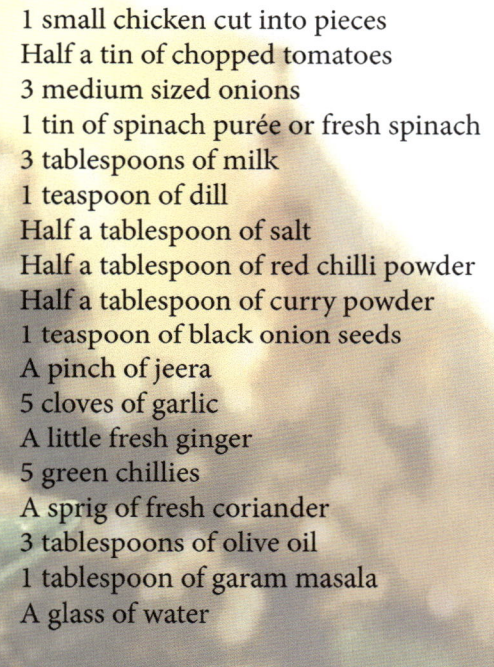

Dean Gorré
Lamb Biryani

"Biryani has always been a favourite of mine so to learn from a top chef was a chance in a million!"

Dean Gorré, football coach

Ingredients:

1¼ cups of basmati rice
2 garlic cloves
1 inch of ginger
4 cloves
2 green cardamom pods
Half teaspoon black pepper corns
1 teaspoon cumin seeds
1 teaspoon coriander seeds
1 inch piece cinnamon stick
1 teaspoon saffron strands in tepid water (let it soak)
1 tablespoon olive oil
1 medium sized onion
¼ teaspoon chilli powder
1lb boneless lamb cut into cubes
6floz natural yoghurt
2 tablespoons (golden raisins) sultanas
1oz flaked toasted almonds

Method:

1) Bring a large saucepan of salted water to the boil. Add the rice and boil for 6 minutes. Drain and set aside.
2) Grind together all the garlic, ginger, cloves, cardamom pods, pepper corns, cumin, coriander and cinnamon.
3) Combine the saffron and water and set aside. Heat the butter or olive oil in a large saucepan and add the sliced onion. Fry until golden brown then add the ground spice mix and chilli powder. Stir for a few minutes and add the lamb. Cook until evenly browned.
4) Add the yoghurt, stirring all the time, then add the sultanas and bring to a simmer and let it cook for 50 minutes, stirring inbetween.

Bear Grylls
King Prawn Korma & Garlic Naan

"I felt it was a great cause to put my name to, The Children's Hospital, and I was very touched by Hashim's story. All the best."

Bear Grylls, TV presenter

Ingredients:

2 tablespoons olive oil
2 medium sized onions
1 inch fresh ginger (crushed)
4 cloves of garlic (crushed)
3 green chillies
2 teaspoons salt
1 teaspoon red chilli powder
1 teaspoon ground cumin
1 teaspoon ajwain seeds
¼ teaspoon turmeric
¼ pint coconut milk
1 tablespoon tamarind paste
2lb uncooked, shelled king prawns
1 glass of water
Fresh coriander

Method:

1) Soften the chopped onions in the olive oil and add the ginger and garlic.
2) Add the green chillies finely chopped and all of the spices and the tamarind paste. Stir thoroughly as this forms the masala.
3) Add the glass of water and coconut milk and simmer for 15 minutes once you have brought the mixture to the boil.
4) Wash the prawns and add to the masala and cook for 5 minutes or until the prawns are cooked.
5) Garnish with the fresh coriander when serving.

Jason Done
Chicken Tikka Masala

> *"My all time favourite curry!"*
>
> Jason Done, actor (Waterloo Road)

Ingredients:

2lb chicken breasts, cubed (2cm cubes)
2 tablespoons olive oil
2 medium sized onions
3 garlic cloves (crushed)
Inch of ginger root (crushed)
1 lemon
2 small chillies (green)
150ml natural yoghurt
2 teaspoons cumin seeds
2 tablespoons tomato puree
100 ml coconut milk
50ml crème fraiche
Teaspoon garam masala
2 teaspoons salt
1 teaspoon red chilli powder

Method:

1) In a large bowl add the half the chopped onion, garlic and ginger.
2) Add half of the lemon juice and cumin and natural yoghurt to form the marinade. Add the cubed chicken and leave to marinate in the refrigerator for at least 2 hours.
3) Soften the remaining onion, garlic and ginger and add the green chillies. Stir in the tomato puree, salt and chilli powder.
4) Add the coconut milk and simmer for 20 minutes.
5) Add the crème fraiche and the rest of the lemon juice.
6) Blend the sauce with a hand held blender.
7) Thread the chicken cubes onto wooden skewers and cook under the grill for 15 minutes turning frequently.
8) Add the cooked chicken cubes to the blended sauce and stir. Simmer for 5 minutes. Stir in the garam masala and garnish with coriander.

Tupele Dorgu
Chicken Korma

Tupele Dorgu, actress (Coronation Street)

Ingredients:

3 Medium sized onions
3 tablespoons olive oil
Tin 400gm chopped tomatoes
4 cloves of garlic crushed
Inch of ginger, crushed
2lb boneless chicken breast (cubed to 2cm)
2 tablespoons cashew nuts (chopped)
Half tablespoon salt
1 teaspoon red chilli powder
¼ teaspoon yellow food colouring
¼ teaspoon turmeric
¼ teaspoon single cream
1 teaspoon garam masala
Sprig of fresh coriander
1 glass of water

Method:

1) Soften the chopped onions in the olive oil.
2) Add the chopped tomatoes, garlic and ginger.
Stir thoroughly.
3) Add the salt, chilli powder, yellow food colouring,
turmeric and bring to the boil with 1 glass of water.
4) Add the chicken and cashew nuts and cook for 5
minutes stirring regularly.
5) Turn the heat slightly down and stir in the cream
and simmer for 10 minutes, stirring once in the
middle – i.e. after five minutes.
6) Stir in the garam masala and check to see if the
chicken is tender.
7) Garnish with fresh coriander.

Jimi Harkishin
Keema Matr

> "*I feel honoured to be helping this great hospital.*"
>
> Jimi Harkishin, actor (Coronation Street)

Ingredients:

2lb minced lamb
400gms tin of chopped tomatoes
2 medium sized onions
Half tablespoon salt
1 teaspoon chilli powder
1 teaspoon haldi
1 teaspoon cumin seeds
5 cloves of garlic
An inch of ginger
4 green chillies
3 tablespoons olive oil
8oz peas
2 glasses of water
Fresh coriander and garam masala

Method:

1) Chop the onions and brown in the olive oil. Add
the cumin seeds and let pop for a few minutes.
Add the spices and then the tomatoes, ginger and
crushed garlic and 1 glass water.
2) Add the minced lamb and cook for 15 minutes on
a low heat.
3) Increase the heat to full and stir well and "pun".
4) Add the peas, green chillies and the other glass of
water and let it all cook until the peas are done.
5) Add the coriander and garam masala to garnish.

Fiona Bruce

Southern Indian Fish Curry

> "I was very touched by the whole story and wanted to help in any way, so doing this was easy."

Fiona Bruce, newsreader and TV presenter

Ingredients:

2 tablespoons olive oil
2 medium sized onions
Half tin chopped tomatoes
2 cloves garlic crushed
2cm ginger finely chopped
400ml coconut milk
3 cardamom pods with the skin discarded- use only the seeds
Teaspoon cumin
Teaspoon cinnamon
2 teaspoons red chilli powder
1 teaspoon turmeric
2 teaspoons salt
3 tablespoons water
700 gms white fish fillet cut into 2cm cubes
Fresh coriander

Method:

1) Crush the cardamom seeds, add the cumin, cinnamon, chilli powder, turmeric and salt and mix to a paste with the water.
2) Soften the finely chopped onion, garlic and ginger for a few minutes. Then add the chopped tomatoes, ginger and garlic.
3) Add the spice paste and cook for a few minutes stirring continuously.
4) Add the coconut milk and bring to the boil.
5) Add the fish and let simmer for 20 minutes stirring occasionally.
6) Garnish with the fresh coriander.

Nigel de Jong
Coconut Prawn Curry

"Great curry for footballers everywhere!"

Nigel de Jong, ex-footballer

Ingredients:

800 grams of large uncooked prawns
Half tin 200gms chopped tomatoes
2 medium sized onions
Inch of ginger
2 cloves of garlic (crushed)
30 ml/1 floz coconut milk
2 tablespoons olive oil
Teaspoon ground turmeric
Teaspoon chilli powder
Half teaspoon five-spice powder
Half teaspoon ground cumin
¼ teaspoon of caster sugar
1 teaspoon salt
Sprig of fresh coriander
100ml water

Method:

1) Soften the chopped onions in the olive oil and the garlic, ginger and the tin of chopped tomatoes. Mix thoroughly.
2) Add the spices and salt and let it cook for 5 minutes.
3) Add the coconut milk and sugar and 100ml water and add the prawns and cook gently for 20 minutes or until the prawns are cooked.
4) Garnish with coriander when serving.

Mike Toolan
Chicken Karahi

"I hope this book sells millions and I wanted to help this great cause in whatever way I could. Good luck, Parveen!"

Mike Toolan, Key 103 radio presenter

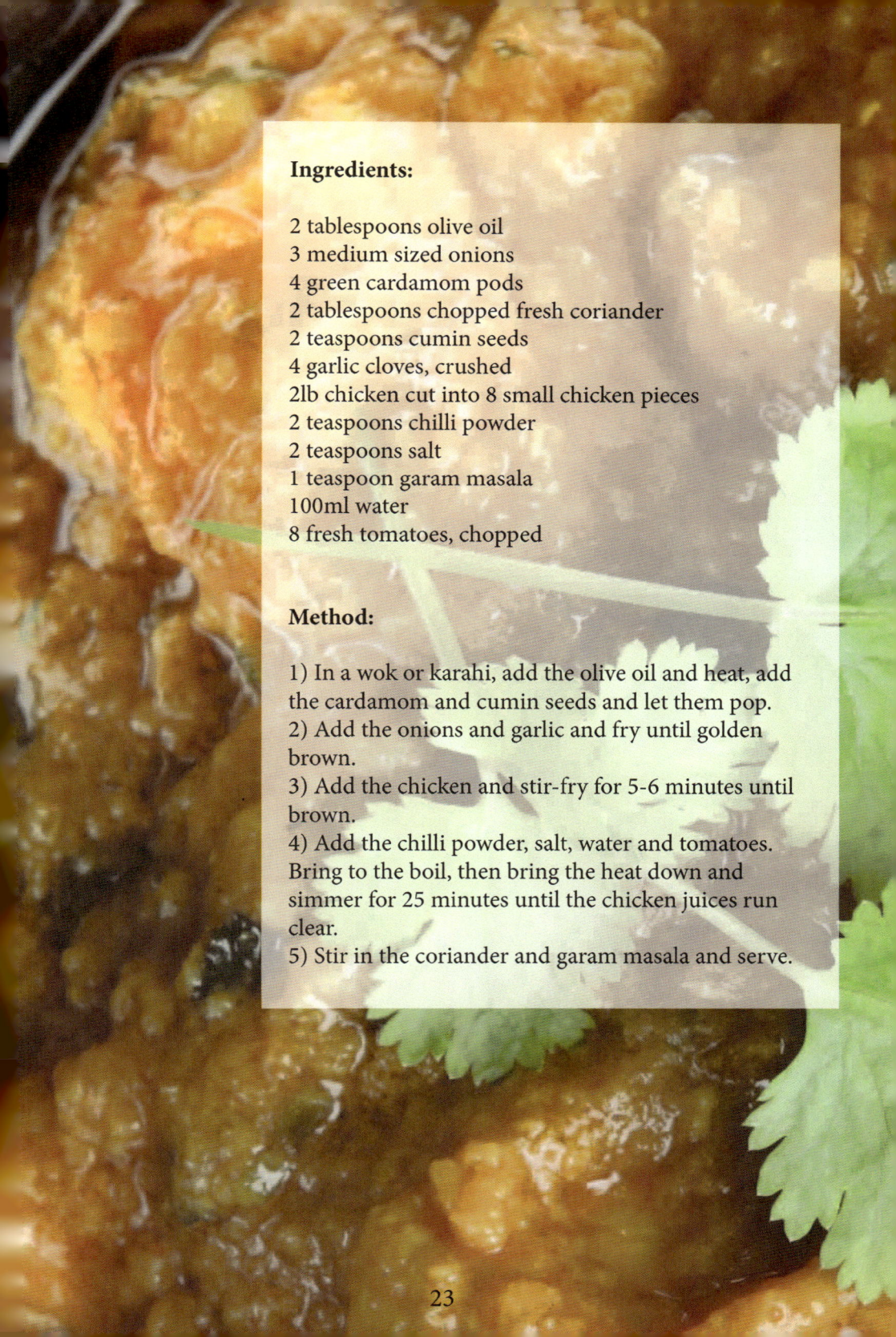

Ingredients:

2 tablespoons olive oil
3 medium sized onions
4 green cardamom pods
2 tablespoons chopped fresh coriander
2 teaspoons cumin seeds
4 garlic cloves, crushed
2lb chicken cut into 8 small chicken pieces
2 teaspoons chilli powder
2 teaspoons salt
1 teaspoon garam masala
100ml water
8 fresh tomatoes, chopped

Method:

1) In a wok or karahi, add the olive oil and heat, add the cardamom and cumin seeds and let them pop.
2) Add the onions and garlic and fry until golden brown.
3) Add the chicken and stir-fry for 5-6 minutes until brown.
4) Add the chilli powder, salt, water and tomatoes. Bring to the boil, then bring the heat down and simmer for 25 minutes until the chicken juices run clear.
5) Stir in the coriander and garam masala and serve.

John Thomson

Makhan Chara (Buttered Chicken)

John Thomson, actor and comedian

Ingredients:

4oz butter
2 cloves garlic crushed and half inch ginger crushed.
2 small onions finely chopped
Half tin chopped tomatoes
Teaspoon ground coriander
Teaspoon ground cumin
Half teaspoon turmeric
2 teaspoons red chilli powder
2 teaspoons salt
2lb boneless chicken thighs or breast fillets, cut into 2cm cubes
1 cup double cream
2 tablespoons coconut milk
1oz roasted almonds and fresh coriander

Method:

1) Brown the onions in the melted butter.
2) Add the tomatoes and garlic and ginger and all the spices.
3) Add the chicken pieces and cook for 5 minutes.
4) Add the cream and coconut milk, bring to the boil and let it simmer for 35 minutes or until the chicken is tender.
5) Garnish with roasted almonds and fresh coriander.

Amir Khan
Karahi Chops

Amir Khan, boxer

Ingredients:

3lb lamb chops
4 medium sized onions
2 tablespoons olive oil
1 tin of chopped tomatoes (500 gms)
Small pot of plain yoghurt
Half tablespoon salt
Half tablespoon red chilli powder
2 teaspoons haldi
2 teaspoons cumin seeds
8 cloves of garlic
2 inches of ginger
1 pint of water
Fresh coriander
1 teaspoon garam masala

Method:

1) Brown the chopped onions in the olive oil.
2) Add all the spices and ginger and garlic.
3) Add the washed chops to the masala and add the pint of water.
4) Let them cook for about 45 minutes, then add the plain yoghurt and "pun" the chops.
5) Add the fresh coriander and garam masala.

Ray Ranson
Chicken Bhuna

> *"Hashim is a remarkable boy and I would have done anything to help his hospital."*
>
> Ray Ranson, ex-footballer

Ingredients:

1 medium sized chicken cut into pieces
Tin chopped tomatoes (400gms)
3 medium sized onions
Half tablespoon of salt
Half tablespoon of red chilli powder
Half tablespoon of curry powder
Pinch of jeera
5 cloves of garlic
Inch of fresh ginger
5 green chillies
Sprig of fresh coriander
3 tablespoons of olive oil
1 tablespoon of garam masala
Glass of water

Method:

1) Chop the onions and brown in the olive oil until golden brown.
2) Add the tomatoes, crushed garlic and ginger, all the chilli powder and green chillies, salt, curry powder, jeera and stir thoroughly.
3) Add the washed chicken pieces with the glass of water and put on full heat for 5 minutes.
4) Lower the heat and leave for 15 minutes to cook.
5) Increase the heat to full and "pun" the chicken.
6) Add the garam masala and coriander to garnish.

Julie Hesmondhalgh

Vegetarian Balti Rogan Josh

> *"What a miracle boy!"*
>
> Julie Hesmondhalgh, actress
> (Coronation Street)

Ingredients:

2 tablespoons olive oil
2 medium sized onions chopped
8oz chopped tomatoes
1 teaspoon black onion seeds
4oz courgettes (sliced)
4oz potatoes (cubed)
Small aubergine (cubed)
Half pint of water
2 crushed garlic cloves
1 teaspoon red chilli powder
1 teaspoon salt
1 teaspoon turmeric
2 fresh green chillies
1 teaspoon garam masala
A sprig of fresh coriander to garnish

Method:

1) Brown the chopped onions in the balti or large wok and add the chopped tomatoes, black onion seeds and garlic.
2) Add all the spices and the water.
3) Then add all the vegetables and green chillies, bring to the boil and let simmer for 15 minutes or until the potato is cooked.
4) Add the garam masala and fresh coriander to garnish.

Sir Richard Branson
Chicken Pilau Rice

Sir Richard Branson

Ingredients:

1 medium sized chicken
3 medium onions
8oz butter
2 tablespoons of cumin
5 sticks of cinnamon
5 large cardamoms
1 tablespoon black peppercorns
6 green chillies
9 cloves of garlic
1 inch of fresh ginger
Small pot of plain yoghurt
5 glasses of Basmati rice
6¼ glasses of water
2 tablespoons of salt

Method:

1) Brown the onions in the butter and add all the dry spices.
2) Add chicken, garlic, ginger and green chillies.
3) Pun the chicken on a high heat for 20 minutes and add the plain yoghurt and pun again for a few minutes.
4) Add the water and let the mixture come to the boil. When it is boiling add the drained rice.
5) Evaporate the water off and do the dam* for 20 minutes.

*Dam – dampen a tea towel and fasten around the lid to create a rice cooker.

Sir Trevor McDonald
Lamb Bhuna

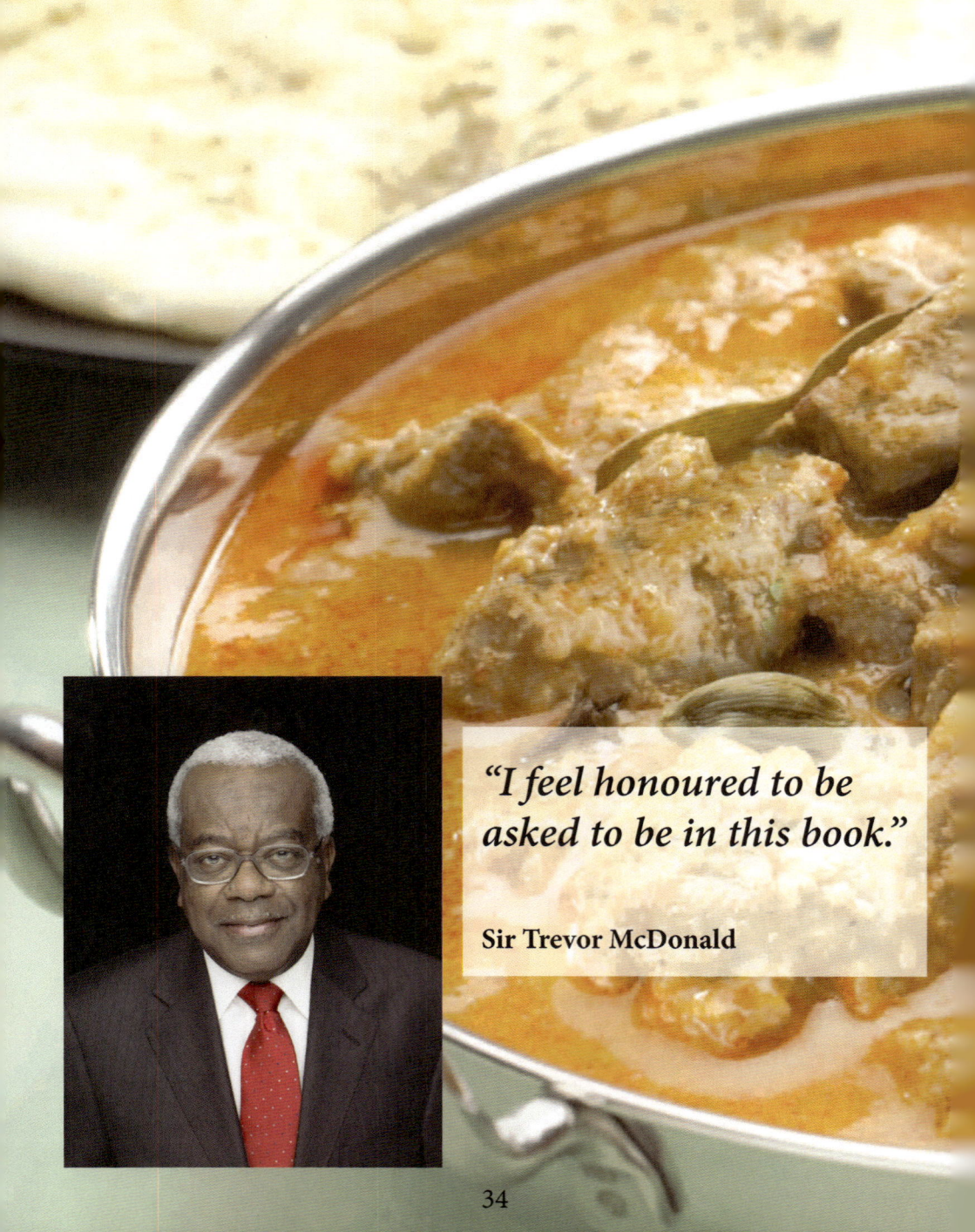

> *"I feel honoured to be asked to be in this book."*
>
> Sir Trevor McDonald

Ingredients:

2lb lamb cut into pieces
400gm tin of tomatoes
3 medium sized onions
Half teaspoon salt
1 teaspoon curry powder
Half teaspoon turmeric
5 cloves of garlic and 1 inch of fresh ginger
5 tablespoons of olive oil
1 tablespoon garam masala
Fresh coriander
Glass of water

Method:

1) Chop the onions into the olive oil, add the tomatoes and all the spices.
2) Add the washed lamb and the glass of water.
3) Let it cook for 40 minutes on a medium heat.
4) Then pun the lamb for 5 minutes or until you can see the fat goblets forming on top of the pan.
5) Add the coriander and garam masala.

Gemma Atkinson
Chicken Rogan Josh

Gemma Atkinson, actress (Hollyoaks)

Ingredients:

2 tablespoons olive oil
3 medium sized onions
3 cloves of garlic (crushed)
400 grams tinned tomatoes (chopped)
2lb boneless chicken
Half tablespoon red chilli powder
Half tablespoon salt
¼ teaspoon turmeric
Teaspoon garam masala
Small pot of yoghurt
Fresh coriander to garnish
1 glass of water

Method:

1) Brown the onions in the olive oil and add the crushed garlic and chopped tomatoes.
2) Add the spices and the glass of water and stir thoroughly and cook for 5 minutes.
3) Add the washed chicken and cook for a further 20 minutes.
4) Add the yoghurt and let it simmer for 5 minutes.
5) Add the fresh coriander and garam masala to garnish.

Sir Michael Parkinson
Bombay Potatoes

> *"The samosas were amazing, I hope the Bombay Potatoes are just as good. What an incredible child, I would love to help."*

Sir Michael Parkinson

Ingredients:

2 tablespoons olive oil
1 inch fresh ginger (crushed)
2 cloves of garlic (crushed)
1 tablespoon cumin seeds
500gms/1lb potatoes, peeled and cut into 2 cm
cubes and boiled
2 green chillies, finely chopped
2 teaspoons lime juice
1 teaspoon salt
Sprig of fresh coriander

Method:

1) In a large frying pan heat the olive oil and add the
crushed ginger, garlic and cumin seeds. Stir-fry for
2 minutes.
2) Add the potatoes and chilli, salt and lime juice
and sauté for 6-8 minutes or until the potatoes are
golden brown.
3) Garnish with fresh coriander.

n.b. These potatoes go very well as an accompani-
ment to chicken and fish dishes.

Leona Lewis
Chickpea Curry

> *"I would love to help this wonderful hospital, and even better I get to learn how to make my favourite curry!"*

Leona Lewis, singer and X Factor winner

Ingredients:

250 grams chickpeas (tinned)
2 medium sized onions
Half a tin of chopped tomatoes (200 gms)
2 cloves of crushed garlic
Half an inch of ginger
1 teaspoon salt
Half a teaspoon red chilli powder
1 green chilli
Half teaspoon of haldi (turmeric)
2 glasses of water
Sprig of fresh coriander
1 tablespoon olive oil

Method:

1) Brown the onions in the olive oil and add the tomatoes, crushed garlic and the ginger.
2) Add the salt, chilli powder and green chilli chopped, turmeric and add the water and let it cook for 5 minutes.
3) Add the chickpeas and fresh coriander and let it cook for a further 20 minutes.
4) Serve with freshly boiled rice.

John O'Shea
Lamb Rogan Josh

"I don't think Sir Alex Ferguson would be too happy with me chopping onions a night before a match but when I tell him it was for the Royal Manchester Children's Hospital, he'll understand!"

John O'Shea, footballer

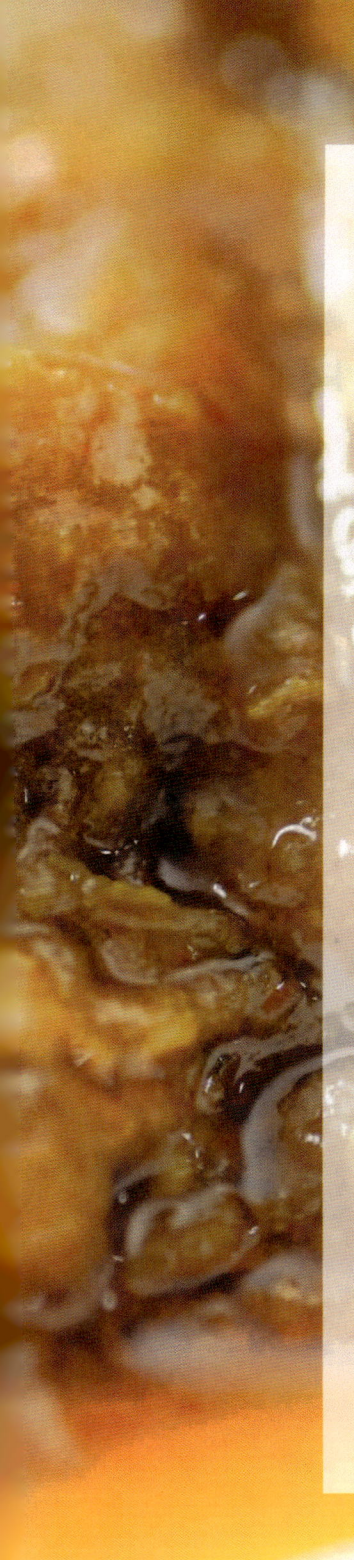

Ingredients:

3 tablespoons olive oil
2 medium sized onions
1 inch ginger and 5 cloves of garlic (crushed using mini blender or garlic press)
5 cloves
4 cinnamon sticks
1kg/2¼ boneless leg of lamb cut into 2cm cubes
275g plain yoghurt
1 tablespoon red chilli powder
1 tablespoon sugar
Half teaspoon saffron strands
5 tablespoons Khoya or full fat milk powder
Half tablespoon salt
Half pint water
Fresh coriander
1 teaspoon garam masala

Method:

1) In a large pan add the 3 tablespoons of olive oil.
2) Add the chopped onion and brown.
3) Add the crushed ginger and garlic, cloves, cinnamon sticks, lamb, plain yoghurt, chilli powder and salt. Cook on a very low heat for 20-25 minutes. All the juices will evaporate and then you cook stirring the meat round for 15 minutes until the meat turns a reddish brown in colour.
4) Add the sugar and saffron to the water and pour over the lamb mixture and cook again on a very low heat for 20 minutes.
5) Add the khoya or milk powder and cook on a low heat for another 10 minutes. It is now ready to eat.
6) Garnish with coriander leaves and garam masala.

Sally Dynevor
Matr Paneer

"I always wanted to know how to make a curry properly and now was my chance to learn from The Curry Queen of Hale. How could I say no to the invitation to Parveen's kitchen?"

Sally Dynevor, actress (Coronation Street)

Ingredients:

250gms paneer – cubed
2 medium sized onions
400gm tin of chopped tomatoes
3 cloves of garlic (crushed)
Inch of ginger (crushed)
Half tablespoon salt
1 teaspoon red chilli powder
Half teaspoon turmeric
Half teaspoon black onion seeds
Pinch of jeera   *Cumin seeds*
2 glasses of water
1lb peas
1 teaspoon garam masala
2 tablespoons olive oil
Fresh coriander

Method:

1) Brown the chopped onions in the olive oil, add the tomatoes, crushed garlic and ginger, salt, chilli powder, turmeric, black onion seeds, jeera and the glass of water. Cook for five minutes.
2) Add the cubed paneer and cook for another 20 minutes on a low heat.
3) Add the peas and the other glass of water and cook for five minutes.
4) Add the garam masala and fresh coriander to garnish.

about the author.

Parveen Ahmed is a mother of five from Hale, who is known for her delicious and authentic Indian cuisine.

Parveen was chosen to take part in the ITV series 'There's No Taste Like Home', where celebrity chef Gino D'Acampo helps cooks recreate a family recipe for paying diners. Parveen came runner up in the show, and it was Gino who first dubbed her 'The Curry Queen'.

Parveen also runs cooking classes, the Taj Mahal Cookery Club, which attracts locals to come and learn how to make authentic Indian food. She used to write a weekly food column for Cheshire Magazine, as well as writing for Living Edge magazine and being published in Family Circle and Cheshire Life magazines. Parveen is currently a food columnist for Hale and Bowden magazine. She was nominated for Cheshire Woman of the Year 2012.

www.curryqueen.co.uk

Printed in Great
Britain
by Amazon

32378724R00026